THOUGHTS, POEMS
and
FREE VERSE

THOUGHTS, POEMS
and
FREE VERSE

DION HENRY

XULON PRESS

Xulon Press
2301 Lucien Way #415
Maitland, FL 32751
407.339.4217
www.xulonpress.com

Paperback ISBN-13: 978-1-66283-435-6
Ebook ISBN-13: 978-1-66283-436-3

DEDICATION

To God, who created me in His image.

To my mother, Mattie Carol, who gave me life and freedom to be. To the mothers of my children, Christina and Debra. To my children, Rasheem and Manijah. Last but not least, to my grandchildren, Marccel, Khloe, and RJ. If it weren't for you, I wouldn't have a reason.

TABLE OF CONTENTS

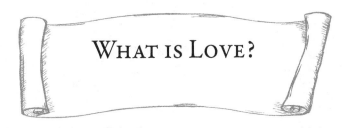

WHAT IS LOVE?

Love is a four-letter word; it doesn't necessarily express what is written in books and novels.

It doesn't give you that warm snuggly feeling when it comes from someone who has spewed like a piece of property.

It doesn't make your heart leap for joy when it comes from someone who just treated you like a piece of property.

It doesn't make you smile when you've been demoted from wife to servant.

It doesn't make up for the sacrifices you have made to forfeit your dreams to be an insignificant part of someone else's dream.

What is Love?

I want to know... What is Love?

TRUE MASTER

I am the master of my destiny. Who
    but me, can dictate where, what, why,
        when, how, I should or should not be?

I am a king born of royal blood.
    Therefore, I must be the master of me.
        I am the decider in all things
            Concerning D.

You can incarcerate my body,
    you can throw away the key. My mind is
        impenetrable, immune to your iniquity.

I'm on an eternal quest for knowledge,
    so I'll always be free.
        Captain of the ship, lord of the ring.

So you see, I be who I say I be:
    Dion M. Henry, master of all
        things me.

D.M.H
01/06/2012

Next Breath

How I feel about you is how I feel about my next breath:
I need it, and I can't live without it.
I'd be lost to oblivion, surrounded by darkness,
no if, ands, or buts about it.
I don't know how this thing of ours started, but I'm happy to the point
where I just want to shout it...

How I feel about you is how I feel about my next breath:
without it, without you, there'd be nothing left.
In the darkness of day and feeling bereft, you crept into my life and
into my chest
my heart is content and the darkness has left.
Without you, my dear, I wouldn't need a next breath...

How I feel about you is how I feel about my next breath:
imagine me in bed sick with strep.
I'd write the words "I love you" until you could feel
my breath on your ears and neck.
The last time we had sex, in my memory it's fresh.
I love you, sweet lady,
on that you can bet.
Without you, there's nothing left.
There's no need for a next breath...

D.M.H
04/15/2009

Trace of Life

As the hands of time pass me by,
I see traces of my life in places I can hardly describe.
Pieces of myself in places riddled with crime.
Lived life fast so I could wine & dine.
The fine young thing down the block
I claimed as mine.
We all know there comes a time
you reap what you sow, you gotta do your time.
Faces start to fade, but traces still remain.
The more rapidly things change,
the more they stay the same.

D.M.H
01/13/2012

WHERE IS THERE?

Before I was here, I was there.
Funny thing is, I don't know where is there.
Everything I did, everything I saw
was at break-neck pace.
Never took time to enjoy one place.
New York, Va, Californ-I-AY.
As I think about it now, there's
a cloud that shrouds
disappointment in the eyes of those
that remember.
My boy Clef once said I'll be gone
till November.
Funny how it seems some things
are gone and others you remember.
Before I was here, I was there,
and it's the middle of December.

D.M.H
12/13/2011

FREE

Freedom is mine. At no time will I be blind to the fact that doing time is whack,

selling nicks and dimes of crack,

living high on the hog off the backs of Blacks.

Crime rates crazy, will I be next to get blamed and be Swazy?

Hell nah! I'm too sharp for that.

I'm my mother's baby, Pop Dukes wasn't there,

so Mattie Carol raised me.

Freedom is mine. I gotta be who I be.

No way, not me, never again will I be

too blind to see that Toten' guns and make-in runs ain't who I be.

Freedom is mine. The Clouds have cleared and now I see.

D.M.H.
Rev. 01/23/2012

BE PROUD

Stand tall and be proud of from which you came.
My ancestors were kings and queens. Can you say the same?
One false move and the whole game can change
from the downfall of man rises an empire through the scam.
Neanderthals, Homo Erectus, Cro-Magnon – man.
Though they wouldn't last long cause their brains
were too small. Never meant to reign; just a link in the chain.
So stand tall and be proud of from which you came,
cause we are on the rise and will reign again

D.M.H.
Rev. 02/04/2012

DEAREST DAUGHTER

I'm wishing you the best at this blessed time of year.
Not a day goes by don't I wish I was there.
Near to your ear, so I can tell you how much I love and care
my fear of not knowing you appears more clear
as the years go by and I'm still not there.
Whenever you're ready, I'm here sincere.
I love you, now and always.

Merry Xmas and Happy New Year!

Love Daddy

D.M.H.
12/20/2011

SEE ME FREE

If God is the God that I know His to be,
    He will see me free.
Cause Lord knows it's my son I want to see.
So I pray to my Lord every night before I sleep,
    on my hands & knees I'll be,
        until my Lord sets me free.

D.M.H.
05/11/2000

WHERE AM I?

This place that I'm in is unlike any other
    where men kill for a chance at his lover.

No place like this have I seen in my life
    where the necessities of life is a thump
    game and a knife.

This place that I'm in there are no holds barred.
    If you can't hold your own, you accumulate scars.

No place like this have I seen in my life
    where men look like men, but live like a wife.

This place that I'm in is unlike any other
    where the souls of men are sold for the life
    of another brother...

    Where am I?

D.M.H.
06/07/2000

My Place

At night when it's quiet
    and I could hear myself breathe,
        I take trips to places where
            there's nobody, but me.

My favorite trip is to this place
    with no
        signs, no cars, no noise, no phonelines.

It's a beautiful place with a Malibu breeze
    I often think it's heaven, but nah,
        it can't be.

Maybe it's just a place where there's nobody,
    but me...

D.M.H.
05/12/2000

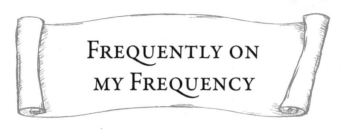

FREQUENTLY ON MY FREQUENCY

Frequently thoughts of you cloud my mind.
Frequently I think I'm out of my mind.
Frequently I think of you to pass the time.
Frequently I think of you, thinking of me,
with hopes of you, one day, frequently
sharing my frequency.

D. M O E T
05/11/2000

I Often Have Thoughts of You

Thoughts of you often cross my mind.
Thoughts of you often make me cry.
Often thoughts of you make me wonder why.
Often thoughts of you leave me feeling blind.
Thoughts of you are often thoughts of you thinking
of me. Thoughts of you to me are like food:
I can't live without thoughts of you.

D. MOET
05/11/2000

THEN AND NOW

We first met at the Pond Lily Motel,
    destined to be my wife.

No one could tell we fell deeply
    in love, together everyday
        like a hand in a glove.

Every chance we got we made love
    like rabbits.

But our love is no more, cause
    together we reeked havoc.

D. M O E T
05/11/2000

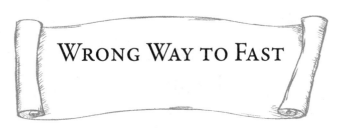

WRONG WAY TO FAST

An A and B student found his way to the street.
    In a rush to be a man and stand on his own two feet.
        Little did he know, it was his destiny he'd soon meet.

Slinging drugs and toting guns, he had to admit
sometimes it was fun. The fun came to a stop, the

    day he got shot. He was almost killed, he was shot
        by a cop, near death experience. In recovery he came

around. During the operation, he watched his life

    go down from across the room. No, he didn't die, but
        his destiny he did meet. He's a preacher in prison
and for the rest of his days, that's where he'll be.

D.M.H.
06/12/2000

ENVIRONMENTAL PRODUCT

What u no abut sellin' drugs and bussin' slugs,
    so u and da fam can eat?

Going to jail, living in a cell, living life
    to the same beat, as u was in the
    street.

Surrounded by poverty, connivery, dope sales,
    and thievery.

Yu start to tell yourself, they can't expect
    anything different from me.

D.M.H.
08/22/2003

SLAVE

As days turn to nights and nights to days, I can't help but to wonder how long I've been a slave. All of my life. I'd most of the time say slavery isn't always about balls and chains. You see, I had a different master. His name was cocaine.

I didn't use it. I sold it. It's damn near the same. You smoke that shit and you chasing a dream; you sell that shit and you chasing that queen.

We were all slaves, me and the dealers. I knew even the crackheads we sold our shit to. Now I sit in prison for some shit I didn't do. Days turn to nights and nights turn to days, all because I chose to be a slave.

D.M.H
06/12/2000

Right Way
Wrong Time

The Lord is my shepherd.
       The book is my light.

Some choose to run,
       but I'm going to fight.

The ways of the world,
       we know they're not right,

But we're deaf, dumb and blind,
       so we shun the bright light.

D.M.H.
05/14/2000

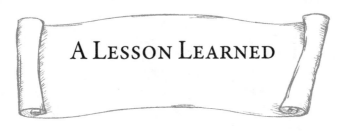

A LESSON LEARNED

Alone we can do so little, but together we can

    conquer the world. The sad thing is, I learned this

too late. I've already lost what I had and she's

    found a new mate. We all have obstacles to conquer,

and Lord knows I have mine, but she will conquer

    the world by a side that's not mine.

D.M.H
05/29/2000

PAST AND PRESENT LOVE

I finally fell in love
    with someone my heart was dreaming of.

It was like heaven came to earth when I fell in
    love with you.

We were happy for a while,
    then I saw the change in your eyes:
    you weren't happy anymore.

Tell me how a thing that brings such joy
    can bring such pain.

How can a love that feels so right
    be so wrong?

I never want to feel the pain of losing love again.

I pray that next time things will be better.

They say better to have loved once
    than to never have loved at all.
        Maybe, maybe not!

Anyway, I'm glad I had a chance to love
    you.

D.M.H.
05/22/2000

LOVE IS

LOVE IS...

       friendship

LOVE IS...

       trusting your partner

LOVE IS...

       happiness

LOVE IS...

       knowing without asking

LOVE IS...

       loyalty

LOVE IS...

       spending quality time together

LOVE IS...

       unconditional

D.M.H.
05/21/2000

IMMATURE

Not until your mind is free
  of poisonous thoughts

Will you be able to give your whole self
  unto a meaningful relationship

D.M.H.
08/26/2003

VICTORS AND VICTIMS

To be addicted to something,

    you must give it your all.

        To overcome an addiction,

            you must give him a call,

                and always be conscious

                    some want to see you fall.

D.M.H.
08/26/2003

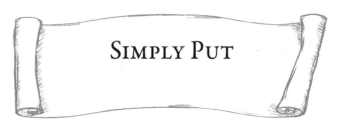

Simply Put

A good dream means there's hope

Somewhere in the midst of this madness

A bad dream means there's

Always the possibility of tragedy

D.M.H.
08/26/2003

MISSING IN ACTION

Three boys,

    A mother on Welfare,

        and a dog.

What's wrong with this picture?

D.M.H.
08/26/2003

One of an Even Number

Morbid are the tales
enshrined within the bindings of this book.
Upon a closer look,
a tortured soul emanating a wayward child
laid to rest is all vengeance
culpable in a person's mind.
I'd cry,
but the blurring of my vision
would surely mark my days.
Not saying that I'm of a calloused heart
for with myself I've made amends,
yet the wrath of lady justice is horrendous
man. I'm weak with determination.
Unabridged are the lessons I've learned
throughout my walk in this hard-knock life,
having lived trife.
I've died twice,
only to resurrect to unpaid debts.
Still morbid are the tales
from a blazing trial on which
my life has took.

By
S. L. J.

ALL I KNOW

A stickup legend was how I attended work,
    for a lack of anything better,
        I proved that two 38s was how I was gonna get mine
        in this fashionable world.

The experience was necessary,
    for the stick and move was a high,
    with a horrifying glaze of fire in my eye.

I thrived off pure fear of winnable thugs.
    The labor is difficult in my line of work;
    your heart has to be secretly private.

Shame to those who can grab a gun and feel power.
    Stickup legends endue the value in their work,
        devour all things,
    never know what the next day will bring.

On each occasion, your name is known among the underworld.
    Consider the end,
        but always on point helps you to defend.

Until the boys in blue get after you,
    most thugs snitch, too.

Stickup legends are born, not made.
    In the eyes of a legend,
        shit will never fade!

By
S. L. J.

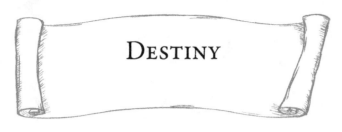

DESTINY

As the buck was passed,
    I thought
it must stop here
    for in a flash
before my eyes,
    I could sense,
taste their fear.
    Scared and cautious,
semi-conscious,
    these niggaz were
draped in sweat.
    So I cocked the hammer,
pulled the trigger,
    and layed their bodies
down to rest.
    Never stressed,
none the less,
    my pulsed increased
its steady rate.
    If life's a quiz,

I passed the test
    engaging them niggaz
to their fate.
    Now I'm respected,
my life's still hectic,
    the jakes are slowly
mounting a case.
    Sky's the limit.
I actually checked it
    and on a poster
saw my face.
    WANTED DEAD OR ALIVE
in big bold letters
    I read the print.
So for now, it's do or die,
    because I'm a true hustler
like Larry Flynt.

By
S. L. J.

TRAPPED

A professional overcrowed,
plans to leave indicates uncertainty.
To forgive is divine,
but nothing's easy.

Mollify the pain,
it equals out to aged mugshots.
Separate the hours,
return lives that were forgot.

Self-assured indicates a subdivision of series,
but the less said is the difference.

Alter its meaning,
stop them from turning ten words into a hundred.
Rewind the play
and be prepared for what's government funded.

Impregnate the law,
split the tin roof of accommodation.
Peace after war,
the reward for all out determination!

By
S. L. J.

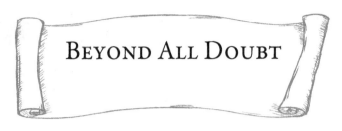

BEYOND ALL DOUBT

It was not proven beyond all doubt,

but I'm pretty sure it was a special reason.

Was it that I'm of a light complexion with curly hair
or was it the fact that the ones who judged me
weren't my peers?

I think I see the facts more clear:
convict all Blacks & Hispanics.
More often than not were guilty,
but more often than not were not guilty

I guess my aging mugshots say another story.

It was reasonable doubt,
but who I was being judged by couldn't see past me.

From being loved to slowly being forgotten,

I ask only one question:

Where's the truth?!

By
S. L. J.

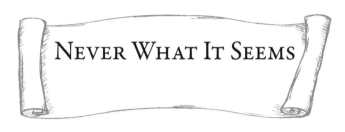

NEVER WHAT IT SEEMS

Trust no appearance for a smile may be notorious.
    Titles are epic.

No need to name the poison, just feel from the chest.
    The world's not wrong,
        just the rest.

Understand thy neighbor,
    for without a doubt the snow is cold.
        Mark its importance and not be sold.

Throughout history our state of being is to proceed
and make better.
    Build a bond.
        Face the east, kneel down, and respond.

Between words are answers,
    a woeful pain held to contain.

The difference is worth noting,
        so maintain!

By
S. L. J.

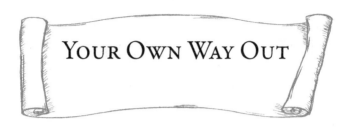

YOUR OWN WAY OUT

Ghetto beauty is like formula,
    a grasp of quality like no other.

A love of deceit that will smother any brother.

The streets are hostile,
    consistent with simplicity,

Whether we're Black, Spanish, or any form of our ancestry.

One way of thought times a million, documented against our own.

An obstacle politicians speak of,
    but let it full blown.

Spoken words cannot be taken back.
    Be proud, resemble your creation.

Blind eyes will never see the light.
    Control your destination!

By
S. L. J.

FOR HER

You're power drivin' with promise,
  an exclusive quality supporting your beauty.

Now that I think back, I double think the nature
of that booty.

Chocolate and conspicuous,
  with a charm that resembles spring.
    Just one of many quantities that you
    always seem to bring.

Lookin' high with thought,
  glowing clouds start to sear.

A reminder of how kind you are.
  I'm happy that you're near!

By
S. L. J.

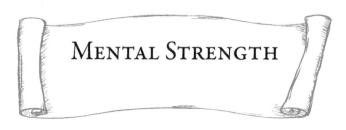

MENTAL STRENGTH

A golden island isn't more breathtaking.
Your clashing wisdom and beauty are distinctions most
    envy and adore.

A drowning portrayed realism,
that traces a flock of cranes across any shore.

You need not stress life's passing grief,
for your personification envies among dozens in many ways.

A capacity rarely related,
        but amazing like a rising spring day,

Hence your strength within.
        Smile upon life's tribulations.

Restore your happiness and spirit with an endless sense
        of determination.

Like a locksmith, only you hold the master key.
        Seek your day's prosperity with a calm
        means of only you can see!

By
S. L. J.

KNOW HOPE

A day and a wakeup

    with determination of being the opposite

      of a hero.

    Some may call me a zero,

    but in my eyes, I'm a ten.

I wonder who said nothing comes easy

    through experience. I know that's a lie.

I don't smoke earth.

    My mom's used enough during my birth,

    but I'm still level headed enough to
make good judgment,

      but I choose not,

        the chief has spoken.

There's three ways to the top:

    the imperative way, the independent way,
and the fast way.

      I chose the last

    I like the fire when my guns blast.

Unfortunately, my actions spoke louder than words,

      My sentence for it all

    numbers & keys.

               Sincerely Yours,
                   S. L. J.

NEVER UNDERSTOOD

The eye of a street philosopher,
treachery of a dark soul.

Inflicted punishment for the nature of his dreams,
all is not all it seems.

Ask if planned to be earnest.
Who was that that said all men were created equal?
The truth is you have to be somebody.
Titles are everything in our zoological world.

I, the new veined messiah, have spoken.

Dear Mr. James,
Do you understand who you are?
Mulatto.
I came from the fruit of an African existence.
The importance of my being
is my persistence.

Capitalize on that, punks!

The lecturer has exited the hall!

By
S. L. J.

Eyes Shut Images

Images from the past.
 Punishment haunted even in a noontime nap.
Fear is overwhelming.
 Sleep within the walls only transpire dreams of
 those who were hurt,
  buried in the dirt.
The panic arrives and I kick with my feet.
 A strange reality that strikes when I'm asleep.
 Shit is deep.
I mask the images with a posterior gain.
 It keeps my smile from looking deranged.
  I deal with shit because in many ways I was wrong
 Most definitely, I prefer to be free,
 but when I close my eyes, I see
 a world not for me.
Deep in the blacks of my eyes there's nothing.
 When I'm awake,
 sometimes I feel all I could take,
but I wiggle free from them thoughts because the poison is myself.
 Images from the past is bad for my health.

By
S. L. J.

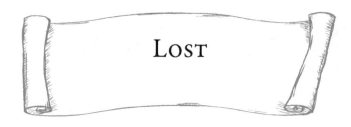

Lost

You don't know me.

You let people think that we're close.
For the most, all you know is that I'm see-through.

You don't know me.

Before I took my first breath, you tried
to abord my death for the shame of my existence.

You don't know me, you don't know life, you don't know shit.

I can remember that time you swung and purposely
hit, adding to my raising scars.

Logical possibility of how poem writing thug
ended up behind bars.

You don't know me.

Since you are a punk, opinion strong,
how the hell you gonna brag now of someone who doesn't belong?

You don't know me.

You only heard of me, a character who is physically
hard. We pump the same blood, but for you I disregard.

You can smile, I can smile, too, like I'm blind and can't see.

A mutual conclusion to a fact that
you don't know me.

By
S. L. J.

IN TIME

You owe me

        Left me in this world lonely

        This high yellow is angry

For moms,

        Outcome, bars, and keys

Coming from me; raising me

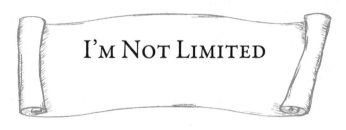

I'M NOT LIMITED

I'm not limited.
In time, in health, in wealth,
in spirit, in hate, in hell,
in heaven, in lust, in jealousy,
in envy, in love, in fear,
in strength, in speech, in reach,
in frared, in speed, in laze,
in case, in care, in there,
in here, in words, in voice,
in relations, in dedications,
in remembrance, in forgiveness,
in nothing, in nowhere, in no how,
in no way, in no shape form.
No, I'm not limited in life!

By
S. L. J.

REMEMBRANCE

When everything was simple,
    we had personable reasons for doing what we did.

We reserved hope for the times
    until we both caught a bid

        in our life. It was no way out.
            We knew this from the gate.
                Cursed & doomed to failure,
                    somehow we found a way to
                relate.
I know you look down and kats still act the same.
    Still smokin' and drinkin', pretending they got game.
        Their lives ain't shit,
            kids we knew still nothing.
            We did what we did.
                Try and build a life and stop frontin'.

Our personal reasons could have floundered to a modern day mind.
    We were winged kids from the street with sight,
        but in a sense remained blind.

They say you kilt yourself,
    but I refuse to listen to them snakes.
        I foresaw our futures
            and our own lives we vowed never to take.

You bared seeds in your journey,
    gave life to two versions of yourself.
        If I shine again, I'll accomplish promise,
            I put that on my health.

E, we still boys beyond just breath
    our selfish reasons carry on.
        Even in our death.

By S. L. J.

PEACE OUT

You was like my bro,
      typical hood kids struggling wit the same woe.
We was thugged out,
        had each other's backs,
       sold cracks,
even joked about futures of being drug kingpins,
but times have changed.
      In so many words, you turned jake,
        so much to the worse
    a condition I can't take.
Altogether, you ruined too much of the game.
    I still got love,
       but can't respect your name.
Nothing we did was ever right
     for our futures was poisoned from the start.
       We kept on going
    and took that snitch shit to the heart.
Since it was me you turned on,
     time shall devour all things.
       Long live the difference.
I loaded, I cocked, I spat.
    There's no winner for us.
       Years spent struggling don't mean shit
    As far away, to empty words,
      a voice of nothing.
       Farewell.   By S. L. J.

RAGE

Common rage replaced by a discreet silence.

    Means of justice capture brave hearts not taught.

Ching-cling

    is the sound of reality,

realization of lives that were sought.

Hate for not being intwined with a role model.

    Evil deeds for lack of confidence to succeed.

        The time is caught.

            Ching-cling

Destruction of innocence before young eyes can really see

    far more power than what we feel is being free.

            Ching-cling

You can silence the rage, but keep building.

            Ching-cling

                Prisons.

                      Sincerely Yours,
                          S. L. J.

ALL AROUND BEAUTY

To phrase a kind heart,
    precisely on this occasion,

With a variety of qualities,
    that always seem amazin'.

You're gentle as feathers fall,
    with essence like baby blue flowers.

A sequence unique as waterfalls,
    but consistent like taking showers.

Since all angels are equal,
    with a beauty that circles no beginning,

Your keenness is everlasting and helps keep my
world from spinning.

Regard and stay strong,
    focused as be.

When you start to feel pressure,

Take a ride and come see me!

By
S. L. J.

SPECIAL

You draw attention like fireworks,
    a person who has much wisdom as well as love.

A routine that's ordinary
    and as precious as the dove.

A tropical purple is how you uplift spirits,
    a metallic strength deep within.

There's so much goodness about you that there's no
place to begin.

Your grace is confidence,
    clear and distant to one's eye,

With knowledge about the Lord that will make anyone
ride the waves that's high.

Equipped with holy happiness years and years through,
    I took on a new role in life,

Half because of you!

By
S. L. J.

ALL AROUND BEAUTY

To phrase a kind heart,
    precisely on this occasion,

With a variety of qualities,
    that always seem amazin,

Your gentle as feathers fall,
    with essence like babyblue flowers,

A sequence unique as waterfalls,
    but consistant like taking showers,

Since all angels are equal,
    with a beauty that circles no beginning,

Your keenness is everlasting & helps keep my
world from spinning,

Regard & stay strong,
    focused as be,

When you start to feel pressure,
    Take a ride & come see me!

By
S. L. J.

PEACE OUT

You was like my bro
    typical hood kids struggling wit the same woe
we was thugged out
           had each others backs
            sold cracks
even joked about futures of being drug kingpins
but times have changed
    in so many words you turned jake
          so much to the worse
    a condition I can't take
Altogether you ruined to much of the game
    I still got love
          but can't respect your name
Nothing we did was ever right
    for our futures was poisoned from the start
          we kept on going
    & took that snitch shit to the heart
Since it was me you turned on
    time shall devour all things;
        LONG LIVE THE DIFFERENCE,
I loaded, I cocked, I spit.
    theres know winner for us
          years spent struggling don't mean shit
    As far away, to empty words,
        a voice of nothing
            farewell

by
S. L. J.

I'm Not Limited

I'm not limited,
in time, in health, in wealth,
in spirit, in hate, in hell,
in heaven, in lust, in jealousy,
in envy, in love, in fear,
in strength, in speech, in reach,
in frared, in speed, in laze,
in case, in care, in there,
in here, in words, in voice,
in relations, in dedications,
in rememberence, in forgiveness,
in nothing, in nowhere, in nohow,
in noway, in no shape form,
no, I'm not limited in life!

by
S. L. J.

LOST

You don't know me
    You let people think that where close
for the most, all you know is that I'm seethrough,
    You don't know me,
        before I took my first breath you tried
to abord my death for the shame of my existence,
You don't know me, You don't know life, You don't know shit,
        I can remember that time you swung & purposely
hit, adding to my raising scars,
        logical possibility of how poem writing thug
ended up behind bars,
    You don't know me,
        since you are a punk, opinion strong,
how the hell you gonna brag now of someone who doesn't belong,
    You don't know me,
        you only heard of me, a character who is physically
hard, we pump the same blood, but for you I disregard,
    You can smile, I can smile too, like I'm blind & can't see,
            A mutual conclusion to a fact that
            You don't know me,

By
S. L. J.

NEVER UNDERSTOOD

The eye of a street philosopher,
treachery of a dark soul,
  Inflicted punishment for the nature of his dreams,
    all is not all it seems,
  Ask if planned to be earnest,
      who was that that said all men were created equal,
the truth is you have to be somebody,
titles are everything in our zoological world,
        I, the new vained messiah have spoken,
        Dear Mr. James,
            Do you understand who you are?
        MULATTO;
  I came from the fruit of a african existence,
the importance of my being,
    is my persistence,
              Capitalize on that punks
            The lecturer has exited the hall!

By
S. L. J.

KNOW HOPE

A day & a wakeup
    with determination of being the opposite
      of a hero
    some may call me a zero
    but in my eyes I'm a 10
I wonder who said nothing comes easy
    through experience I know that's a lie
I don't smoke earth
    my moms used enough during my birth
    but I'm still leveledheaded enough to
    make good judgment,
      but I choose not
        the chief has spoken/
There's three ways to the top
    the imperative way, the independent way,
    & the fast way,
      I chose the last
    I like the fire when my guns blast
unfortunately my actions spoke louder than words
      my sentence for it all
    numbers & keyes;

                sincerely yours...
                    by
                  S. L. J.

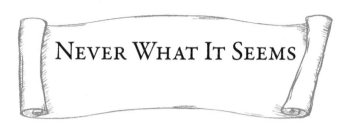

Never What It Seems

Trust no appearance for a smile may be notorious
    titles are epic,

No need to name the poison just feel from the chest,
    the worlds not wrong,
        just the rest,

Understand thy neighbor,
     for without a doubt the snow is cold,
          mark its importance & not be sold,

Throughout history our state of being is to proceed
    & make better,
       build a bond,
         face the east kneel down & respond,

Between words are answers,
    a woeful pain held to contain,

The difference is worth noting,
    So Maintain!...

By
S. L. J.

BEYOND ALL DOUBT

It was not proven beyond all doubt,
but I'm pretty sure it was a special reason,
was it that I'm of a light complexion with curly hair
or was it the fact that the ones who judged me
weren't my peers,
I think I see the facts more clear,
Convict all blacks & Hispanics,
more often then not where guilty
but more often then not where not guilty
I guess my aging mugshots say another story,
IT was reasonable doubt,
But who I was being judged by couldn't see; past me
From being loved, to slowly being forgotten,
I ask only one question,

WHERES THE TRUTH!

BY
S. L. J.

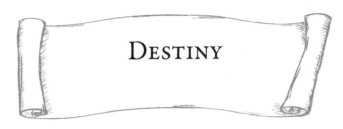

DESTINY

As the buck was passed,
   I thought
it must stop here
   for in a flash
before my eyes,
   I could sense,
taste their fear.
   Scared and cautious,
semi-conscious,
   these niggaz were
draped in sweat.
   So I cocked the hammer,
pulled the trigger,
   and layed their bodies
down to rest.
   Never stressed,
none the less,
   my pulsed increased
its steady rate.
   If life's a quiz,

I passed the test
   engaging them niggaz
to their fate.
   Now I'm respected,
my life's still hectic,
   the jakes are slowly
mounting a case.
   Sky's the limit.
I actually checked it
   and on a poster
saw my face.
   WANTED DEAD OR ALIVE
in big bold letters
   I read the print.
So for now, it's do or die,
   because I'm a true hustler
like Larry Flynt.

By
S. L. J.

TRAPPED

A professional overcrowed,
plans to leave indicates uncertainty.
To forgive is divine,
but nothing's easy.

Mollify the pain,
it equals out to aged mugshots.
Separate the hours,
return lives that were forgot.

Self-assured indicates a subdivision of series,
but the less said is the difference.

Alter its meaning,
stop them from turning ten words into a hundred.
Rewind the play
and be prepared for what's government funded.

Impregnate the law,
split the tin roof of accommodation.
Peace after war,
the reward for all out determination!

By
S. L. J.

ALL I KNOW

A stickup legend was how I attended work,
    for a lack of anything better,
        I proved that two 38s was how I was gonna get mine
        in this fashionable world.

The experience was necessary,
    for the stick and move was a high,
    with a horrifying glaze of fire in my eye.

I thrived off pure fear of winnable thugs.
    The labor is difficult in my line of work;
    your heart has to be secretly private.

Shame to those who can grab a gun and feel power.
    Stickup legends endue the value in their work,
        devour all things,
    never know what the next day will bring.

On each occasion, your name is known among the underworld.
    Consider the end,
        but always on point helps you to defend.

Until the boys in blue get after you,
    most thugs snitch, too.

Stickup legends are born, not made.
    In the eyes of a legend,
        Shit will never fade!

By
S. L. J.

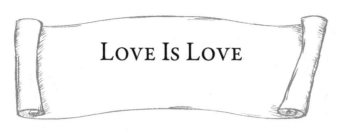

LOVE IS LOVE

We signed those papers, so now you're my ex,
but my love for you will never be met.

I messed up big time, with no one to blame.
So losing my wife is my only shame.

We were young and in love, it was never a game,
but when I lost my wife, it was never the same.

Now I'm plain insane, but to be once loved by
you is my claim to fame.

D-MOET
05/11/2000

THE RIGHT PATH

I sit back and think of all the things I could have been.

I hope it's not too late because I still want to win.

I'll stand before God, if that what it takes,

and swear before Him. Again, I'll never sin.

DMOET
05/11/2000

CPSIA information can be obtained
at www.ICGtesting.com
Printed in the USA
BVHW081135180122
626502BV00003B/338

9 781662 834356